# Rethinking IT

## What needs to be said. How can we solve the IT security problem long term?

Svavar Ingi Hermannsson,

CISSP, CISA, CISM

Svavar Ingi Hermannsson

ISBN-10: 1546410988
ISBN-13: 978-1546410980

# LIMIT OF LIABILITY / DISCLAIMER OF WARRANTY

# CONTENTS

# 1 INTRODUCTION

It's obvious to me that the lack of IT security we are facing today can be solved. It cannot be solved overnight, but we can make a huge impact in a matter of years, assuming everyone pitches in and we get the right people on board.

The solution I envision requires support from every field and industry. We need to address education, policy and regulation proactively. I believe the solution is very simple, but it will require a lot of collaborative hard work.

# 2 BUILDING BRIDGES – FACING THE PROBLEM

I would like to describe the problem as I see it, using a metaphor. Imagine that we have 4.000 builders and engineers designing and implementing bridges in Iceland, and that out of those 4.000 builders, only 1.000 had gotten basic building education at a university level. Now, only 3 of them had gotten an introductory course in bridge building safety. At this point, those 4.000 builders are split up into 500 different groups, where in each group, roughly eight people would be building bridges on their own. Let's assume all of those three people with the basic security knowledge would be given the task to start reviewing bridges already built by the other 3.997 builders (500 different teams). Once the three security assessors complete each assignment they would report the security vulnerabilities they discover. Keep in mind that while older bridges are being reviewed, new ones are constantly being built. When the team of three discovers vulnerabilities in the previously built bridges, which will likely happen frequently, either an attempt will be made to fix them (if they're important enough and there is access to builders) or the builders will simply say that they no longer support this type of a bridge and that you will have to invest in a brand new bridge to replace it costing just as much as the first one, which will fix this particular vulnerability.

I'm not going to go into too much detail on my numbers in this scenario apart from pointing out that as of writing this article, we have only three people registered with a CISSP (Certified Information Systems Security Professional) certificate in the whole country of Iceland, while there are over 70.000 registered companies. Over 1.000 of those companies are registered as IT companies. It is safe to say that there are thousands of people working in in software development and IT infrastructure.

## The old way of trying to address this issue

Most people have been talking about addressing the lack of IT Security issue by training more security people to do inspections of bridges and give remediation suggestions (to reference the previous metaphor).

I have been proposing a completely different approach for the last decade with friends, co-workers as well as in some of my presentations. I've decided to name this method, "The Eyjafjallajökull method". My proposal is to train every single builder in the art of building safety, how to avoid common pitfalls and how to reduce security vulnerabilities and such incidents. We should also continue to train specialized IT security people to do assessments and suggest remediation when vulnerabilities are discovered, but the only way to realistically solve the problem is to educate everybody who are a part of the process. While continuing the previous metaphor, this should include people using and crossing the bridges.

## Every single education level needs to be addressed

- Management
- Software designers / architects
- System & network administrators
- Board members of registered companies
- Auditors
- Legislators
- Primary school, high school, colleges & universities
- Everybody!

# 3 EDUCATING EVERYBODY - BEING PROACTIVE

I believe we need to start being proactive and adjust our curriculum at every school level.

## MBA

How is it possible for someone to graduate with an MBA from an Ivy League business school without having taken a single class covering business security? We expect management, executives and board members of companies to be responsible and accountable for the companies they run. How can we not teach them the basics of business security? Considering the cost of security incidents, it seems obvious that we need executives and general management to understand the importance of IT- and operational security. A board member of a company, or a CEO for that matter, **does not** have to understand technical concepts such as *"What is a buffer overflow"* or *"What is an SQL injection"*. Instead top management should only need to know how to ask the right questions, such as: "Has a vulnerability assessment been performed on our internal network in the past three months (*ideally by an independent third party*)? How many critical vulnerabilities were discovered? Have we started a remediation process for the discovered vulnerabilities?

Furthermore, I would also recommend getting all professors on board, requiring them to take a class on IT and operational security. Following that class, they should be required to assess their own class material (of course with assistance from a professional), and map out potential operational or business security vulnerabilities. The professors should make sure to cover those potential security vulnerabilities with their students along with suggested solutions and mitigation methods.

# Bachelor degrees in business, management and similar

The same thing goes for bachelor degrees. I would recommend a required class on operational security, and also ask the professors to address potential security vulnerabilities in their class material and emphasize it.
Software designers, software architects, software engineers and other programmers

As in every field within our schools and institutions, we need to make sure that the professors, trainers, teacher assistants are aware of IT and operational security threats and how to mitigate them. It would be ideal to have a compulsory class on IT and operational security, but what is more important is that every single class being taught will address potential security threats and appropriate mitigations.

# Bachelor degrees in computer science, electrical engineering, software engineering and similar

Teaching material, such as school books and etc., should not be allowed to contain security vulnerabilities. The simplest programming examples (e.g. writing to a file), should cover race conditions, and how to prevent and minimize such issues. Access control, buffer overflows, format string vulnerabilities, SQL injection vulnerabilities and everything else, should not be present in any source code example, but if they were, they should be required to be marked with big red letters as "**INSECURE CODE**".

When professors and teacher assistants go over homework, students should get minus points (or possibly fail) on their home assignments in case they include security vulnerabilities. It should never be acceptable for a solution to contain security vulnerabilities.

# System & network administrators

No one should be allowed to be a system or network administrator without knowing how to install security patches. At the very least know how to install security updates for the:

- Operating system
- General software updates from manufacturers (e.g. Microsoft/Apple)
- Third party software
- Plug-ins
- Firmware updates
- Other

In the case of network administrators they have to know how to install updates and patches for the firmware of the network equipment they administer.

They also need to understand the implications of not installing updates, patches and fixes. More importantly, their bosses, owners, managers and board members need to understand the importance and possible ramifications it can have on their organization and business if operational security is not maintained.

# Board members of highly regulated companies

In the case of highly regulated companies, they tend to be more monitored and audited compared to SME's. The board members have especially strong accountability. In Iceland today, you are required to have a clean criminal record, pass a character review, and pass an exam to be allowed to sit on the board of such companies. What is currently lacking and could be added without much trouble is business security related questions (with a focus on IT security). Considering the stakes, this should become a requirement, but of course we need to supply the correct training for this as well.

# Auditors

Part of an auditor's role is to check the operational qualifications of a company. In cases where a financial audit is performed for large companies, which rely on IT systems (e.g. for accounting) like most companies do today, an IT audit is performed. Currently those IT audits tend to focus on processes, procedures and making sure that they are followed. The most common processes, which are audited, are for access control, change management, backups, administrative access, separation of duties and etc. All of these are important and say a lot about a company's operational qualifications. Such an audit does not necessarily tell the whole story. I know of cases where those processes and procedures had been documented, and they were being followed, but there was not a single process for installing security updates and patches and they were not being maintained for the operating environment. In other words, it would have been trivial for someone on the internal network to gain administrative access in an untraceable way to the financial system through a security vulnerability in the operating system which was hosting the database system of the accounting software.

Not a single IT Audit should be considered complete without running a vulnerability scanner on the core IT environment. Ideally, the company being audited should have their own vulnerability management program in place and then it's only a matter of checking the results of the latest scans to confirm that the vulnerability management process is being followed. If no vulnerability management program is in place, then the auditor should run a vulnerability scanner on the core infrastructure. If you need to limit the scope of the scan, use a risk based approach.

# Legislators

I think it's important for those who write the law, to have an understanding of the subject they are writing about at each time. I think this should be the case in general, but for my purposes I'm going to focus on IT security. I think we've had plenty of examples that show us that in order for legislation to be effective, non-compliance needs to affect the bottom line of companies. I live in a country, which up until the GDPR, which will take effect in 2018, did not have any financial penalties in the event of a breach of privacy data. There is a famous incident in Iceland, which involved a data breach of an international telecommunication company in November 2013. This was the third time the main webserver of this particular telecommunication company was broken into over a two-year period. The Post and Telecom administration of Iceland concluded that the telecommunication company had broken the nations privacy law, but there's no official penalty. Some private lawsuits were filed but have not been covered in the media.

I think it is safe to assume that had the GDPR taken effect at the time and the telecommunication company in question would have known the potential of being fined 4% of its entire annual turnover. I believe they would have taken action to protect their data prior to the first break in, or at the least after the first break in or after the second break in.

We have lawyers who understand data privacy; hence we now have good privacy laws (the upcoming GDPR). If we had lawyers with a deep understanding of IT security we might have similar requirements to general IT security as well. Technically the current GDPR is focused on technical IT security as well, with regards to implementing acceptable controls, but the way I see it is the GDPR focuses on having a person employed (Data Privacy Officer) which needs to have a deep understanding of Privacy legislation, compliance and etc. It's my belief that if the lawmakers had a similar deep understanding of IT security they would have made the requirement for the same size companies to employ a CISO (not just a DPO). And also require the CISO have a deep understanding of IT security.

I see possibilities of adding more legal requirements to various industries. As mentioned, requiring a CISO for companies, which require a DPO. I would add requirements of basic business security knowledge of executives. This would need to hold hand in hand with the academic approach, we need to have classes available both at undergraduate, graduate and continuous education levels.

Which other law could we possibly introduce? Requiring top management within government to pass certain business and operational security exams? Require anyone who works in critical infrastructure to have had security awareness? Other?

## Business thoughts

If your IT team is unable to manage security updates, patches and the general operation security of your environment, maybe you shouldn't be in this business in the first place?

# 4 THE LOW HANGING FRUIT

To change the entire education system and introduce IT security awareness, where previously there was none, is a huge and complicated task. Most likely it may only be achieved with collaboration between everybody and it will take a lot of hard work.

Do we have some low hanging fruits?

## Cisco and Microsoft

As it turns out, there are cases where IT security material and exams have already been prepared but have not yet been made mandatory. I am only going to mention a couple of such cases which should be familiar to most of the technical people in IT, but may not be familiar to those who do not have a technical IT background. There are other cases out there, but mentioning these two cases should be sufficient to emphasize my point.

## CCNA & MCSA/MCSE

Let us we take a look at a couple of industry certifications, the CCNA from Cisco and the MCSA/MCSE from Microsoft.

# CCNA

Let's start with the Cisco Certified Network Associate (CCNA) certification. Currently, there are around 9 different types of CCNA certifications you can get, so for our purposes, let's focus on the classical CCNA Routing and Switching. You can actually become a CCNA without having covered any IT security to speak off. If you look at the exam topics provided by Cisco the ICND1 and ICND2, they touch on port security and cover three common access layer thread mitigation techniques, but that's it.

While the classic CCNA for routing and switching doesn't cover any IT security worth mentioning, it is important to acknowledge that Cisco does offer a "CCNA **Security**" certification. The IT security topics covered by this exam are pretty impressive and include the following key areas:

- Security concepts
- Secure access
- VPN
- Secure routing and switching
- Firewalls
- Intrusion Prevention System
- Content and endpoint security

When I look at the exam topics for the "CCNA **Security**" certification, I'm impressed. I think Cisco deserves credit for having put this certification in place, but I have a bigger question:

**Why doesn't Cisco make these security topics mandatory for achieving any CCNA certification?**

This emphasizes our current situation. Security is being considered a separate field. If you want to work on a enterprise network, managing the network equipment (e.g. routers and switches), you would get a CCNA in Routing and Switching. If you were going to be a member of the security team, then you would most likely get the CCNA **Security** certificate.

# Imagine

Imagine if the requirements would be changed so that if you wanted to Achieve the "CCNA Routing and Switching" certification, you would not only need to pass ICND1, ICND2 exams but also the security exam. And then and only then would you get your CCNA Certification.

This is in fact my proposal: Make the "CCNA **Security**" exam part, a requirement for any CCNA certification.

# MCSA/MCSE

If we take a look at the Microsoft Certified Solution Associate (MCSA) certification, we have a similar story. If we take a look at the "MCSA Windows Server 2016", you need to pass three exams:

- Exam 70-740/Course 20740A; Installation, Storage, and computer with Windows Server 2016
- Exam 70-741/Course 20741A; Networking with Windows Server 2016
- Exam 70-742/Course 20742; Identity with Windows Server 2016

Interestingly enough, if you look at the details for those exams, they barely touch on IT security. Microsoft, just like Cisco, does offer an exam which covers IT security "Exam 70-744 Securing Windows Server 2016". This is one of ten optional exams you need to pass, in addition to holding an MCSA, in order to become an MCSE. I would argue the same case here, as I did for the CCNA. Make the security part mandatory for any certification. This should be relatively easy to do since all the material and exams already exist.

# 5 DO NOT TEACH PEOPLE HOW TO HACK

I think this is where I and the majority of the people in the IT Security community, which I've talked to about this issue, have disagreed on prior to our conversation (even following our conversations, some may still disagree with me). I believe most if not all IT Security people I have met in the past, and whom I've discussed this issue with, believe we have to teach everybody how to exploit an SQL injection vulnerability or write an exploit for a buffer overflow vulnerability in order for them to understand the implications of such vulnerabilities, and prevent them from occurring and being introduced. I completely disagree. In my opinion it is possible to teach people how to install security updates, how to write secure code and implement a secure operating environment without teaching them how to "hack", break into systems and etc. Please don't get me wrong, I believe full heartedly that offensive classes will give the students a deeper understanding of the subject and I believe we should offer offensive classes, but at the same time I think they should be "optional" as opposed to mandatory and only be offered to people who don't have a criminal record and etc.

# 6 SHOULD WE REQUIRE LICENSES?

## Should we require licenses to operate computers?

If you think about it, if I want to drive a car, I need a driver license, which requires me to pass an exam. If I want to fly an airplane, I need to study and pass an exam. If I want to operate heavy machinery, I need to pass a special exam for that. If I want to own and use a gun, I need to study and pass an exam, as well as get two recommendations and pass a psychological evaluation by a doctor. If you want to work at a pharmacy and mix medication, you're required to be an educated and licensed pharmacist and etc. I'm sure we can come up with plenty other scenarios...

For the previously mentioned scenarios, this makes sense to me. We are talking about situations where the safety of people around you can be threatened if you're not trained or educated in what you are doing.

What I find interesting is that we don't require people to get a license to operate a computer. Ideally, we should be offering different types of computers with different requirements. One type could be similar to tablets or phones (for example an iPad or an iPhone). The device would enforce security updates and would stop working if not updated within an x amount of time. In the case of game consoles for example, maybe you and your parents need to pass a simple class on the importance of hydration, food, sleep, recommended downtime away from the game console and possible health implications; then again, maybe not? At any rate, game consoles should be limited in functionality and may either not require a license or a very basic license. If you want to own and operate a computer where you can do actual software development or run services and servers, serving other people and companies, then you should be required to hold a license and pass an exam which covers operational security. The same should apply for all developers, system administrators and similar.

# Should we require licenses to write software for sensitive infrastructure, health care equipment and everything else?

It's interesting that I cannot simply start making my own car and start selling it, I need to make sure it complies with EU regulation, and most likely have to get it certified and there's a huge process surrounding it. How about if I want to write software for a car? As I'm sure many people have heard of, read about or seen on TV that cars have been hacked remotely even while being driven. Which IT security training did those software developers have? How about the designers and architects of the software? What about the software development teams behind pacemakers, which are in many cases easily hacked and can result in a death? What about election machines and software that could impact the election of a president? I could go on and on talking about critical infrastructure, medical devices and industrial machinery but why stop there? What about software, which handles your personal and private data? Shouldn't that be secure as well?

I realize that out of all the ideas I'm presenting here, this one will be the hardest to implement and may in fact be one of the more unrealistic ones. But since I'm writing this article, I do want to put it out there for people to discuss.

# 7 WHAT WILL NOT BE SOLVED?

To err is human. It doesn't matter how well trained and informed our builders, software developers and architects are, they will make mistakes at some point. If by lack of sleep, trying to rush a product out to meet a deadline or for any other reason, this will happen. Hopefully it will be an exception and not a rule.

Industrial espionage, state sponsored attacks; vulnerability placements and etc. will most likely always exist. This article is not interested in addressing those particular issues. The goal is to focus on the low hanging fruits and bringing the general IT and operational security to a whole new level nationally and internationally.

# 8 POLICY & REGULATION

The ideas I've put forward may sound great, but there's one thing I've learned which is that you need policy, regulation and above all <u>fines</u> to get companies complying.

In Iceland, board members of registered companies are required to pass a competency exam through a personal interview before being allowed to serve on a board. I think this could be great place, to add some operational security related material and make it a part of the examination and a passing requirement.

In the short term, I think it's important to start with the registered companies, and then in the future make similar requirements for board members of unregistered companies as well.

# Impacting the bottom line - fines

It's interesting to have lived in Iceland, where there have been no penalties for computer security break-ins or the leak of personal and private data. As mentioned previously, a telecommunications company in Iceland got hacked in 2013 and personal information of a quarter of the Icelandic population got leaked, this included clear text passwords, usernames, e-mail addresses as well as SMS text messages, which they had been storing in a database. This impacted many people, who were using the same e-mail addresses and passwords for other services. From what I gathered from the media, the data leak came from a database hosted on their webserver and the reason they noticed the hack is that the hacker decided to deface their website and post a link to a copy of the stolen database on twitter. It's also interesting to note that the same webserver had gotten defaced twice before in the previous two years. Was the same data extracted then? Without being posted online? I do not know the answer to that question, but I certainly hope not. Fortunately the European Union has now issued new privacy regulation giving the Data Protection Authority permission to fine a company up to 4% of the global turnover. I am now hopeful for the future of IT Security in Iceland, since this will hopefully force companies to tend to IT security with more care.

# 9 LET'S CHANGE THE WORLD

A decade ago when I was the chairman of an information security focus group within the Icelandic Computer Society I realized one thing. IT security events bring IT security people together. Very frequently you want to reach executives or top management, but even if you organize an IT security event targeted towards them, the odds are that they will send their security guy or one of their system administrators instead of attending themselves.

## Get an IT security related guest lecturer for every type of event

The idea I came up with and offered to other focus groups within the ICS was that for any event they would organize, the information security focus group would be happy to assist with arranging a single IT security focused talk which would be specially customized to their event and the subject being covered.

## Questions, comments and possible collaboration

I enjoy getting constructive feedback and questions, so if you have any questions relating to the material covered in this e-book (or generally related to IT security), please send questions or comments to: **book@eyjafjallajokull.org**

I also enjoy traveling the world and giving talks on cyber security. Feel free to contact me for possible speaking opportunities by email: **speaking@security.is**

Please visit http://www.eyjafjallajokull.org/ for updates relating to this book and the material covered in it.

# 10 COMMON ASSUMPTIONS PEOPLE MAKE

If you are a member of the board of a company, you may assume that information security and business and operation security is taken seriously. Why wouldn't it be? You might make the same assumption if you're the CEO of a company, maybe because you have a CITO whom you believe is experienced. The same could be true for the CFO. In fact, the same could even be true for the CITO and any employee within an organization.

I am going to cover a few controls, which if they have already been implemented at your company or organization, it implies that your IT & Business security is relatively good.

## IT security policy

Has an IT security policy been documented within your organization? Was it approved and issued by executive management, for example the CEO? Has the IT security policy been communicated to the organization's employees? Is the IT security policy reviewed at least once a year in a traceable way?

*If you answered yes to all of the above, you are in good shape. If you don't know the answers to some of these questions, it's a good idea to get answers.*

# IT Security responsibilities

Do you have a CISO (Chief Information Security Officer) at your organization? Has your organization defined and issued responsibilities relating to information security to one or more people? Has your organization defined a point of contact for security vulnerabilities and security incidents that may occur? Make sure you ask and confirm the location of the CISO in the organizational chart; it should be at the top next to all the other CxOs.

*If you answered yes to all of the above, you're in good shape. If you don't know the answers to some of these questions, it's a good idea to get answers.*

Assuming an organization has defined a security officer, there is one measurement, which can tell you how seriously an organization takes its IT security, which is his location within the organizational chart. If an organization has a CISO (Chief Information Security Officer) at the top of its organizational chart, it is a good indicator that this organization is taking IT security seriously. If however you have an IT security officer, who has a boss, who in turn has a boss, who in turn has a boss, then that is a strong indicator that IT security does not have a high priority within that particular organizations.

# Risk assessment & risk treatment

Has your organization defined a process for performing risk assessments? Has an acceptable risk been defined? Did the risk assessment consider IT security related risks? When you performed the risk assessment, did you get input from a subject matter expert, e.g. someone with IT Security credentials (CISSP / CISA/ CISM / etc.)? Has the organization performed a risk assessment at least once a year? Was the risk assessment introduced to top management? Was the risk assessment and approved by top management in a formal and traceable way? Did the risk assessment address ransomware?

Was a risk treatment plan documented in response to all risks, which were outside of the acceptable risk criteria? Were individuals assigned to each control implementation (individual risk treatments)? Were scheduled dates for the risk treatments estimated? Did top management approve the risk treatment plan in a formal and traceable manner?

*If you answered yes to all of the above, you are in good shape. If you don't know the answers to some of these questions, it's a good idea to get answers.*

# Access control process

Has your organization documented and implemented a formal process for access control? Does the process define who is allowed to request creation of user access, modification of user access and closing of user access? Has the process been approved by top management? Is the process audited at least once a year as a part of an internal audit?

*If you answered yes to all of the above, you are in good shape. If you don't know the answers to some of these questions, it's a good idea to get answers.*

# Security Updates

Is a formal process in place to monitor and install security updates for key information systems, all operating systems and network equipment? Are critical security updates installed without any unnecessary delay, once the manufacturer has released them? Are non-critical security updates installed within 90 days of them being released (where 90 days is the upper limit, ideally they should be installed as soon as possible)? Are you sure you're organization is not using software, operating systems or network equipment where the manufacturer has stopped supporting them in the form of security updates and security patches? Is the security update process audited at least once a year as a part of an internal audit?

*If you answered yes to all of the above, you are in good shape. If you don't know the answers to some of these questions, it's a good idea to get answers.*

Do you know how many critical & high security vulnerabilities were discovered within your organization during the last vulnerability scan performed - covering servers, workstations, network equipment and IoT? How many security vulnerabilities were discovered internally and externally?

*If you don't know, it might be enlightening to ask!*

# Vulnerability assessments and penetration testing

Is there a formal process in place to perform vulnerability assessments (looking for security vulnerabilities) within your organization? Are vulnerability assessments being performed at least once every three months on your organization's infrastructure? Does your organization actively address and resolve vulnerabilities, which are discovered? Is the vulnerability assessment process and the resolutions of previously discovered vulnerabilities audited at least once a year as a part of an internal audit? Does your organization perform (or hire someone to perform) a penetration test at least once a year?

*If you answered yes to all of the above, you're in good shape. If you don't know the answers to some of these questions, it's a good idea to get answers.*

# Intrusion Detection System / Intrusion Prevention System

Has your organization installed an IDS or an IPS? Is a qualified person monitoring the IDS/IPS at least daily? Does the IDS/IPS cover your internal network and systems?

*If you answered yes to all of the above, you're in good shape. If you don't know the answers to some of these questions, it's a good idea to get answers.*

# Incident reporting and incident management

Has a formal process for incident reporting and incident management been documented and implemented within your organization? Have these processes been introduced to all employees and contractors which need to know of them? Are employees and contractors encouraged to report security incidents (and other incidents)? Is there a list of reported incidents being maintained? Does management regularly review reported incidents and decide whether action is required to address certain issues? Are the incident reporting and incident management processes audited at least once a year as a part of an internal audit?

*If you answered yes to all of the above, you're in good shape. If you don't know the answers to some of these questions, it's a good idea to get answers.*

# Internal auditing

Has your organization implemented a process for internal auditing where key processes, procedures and policies are audited at least once a year? Are these audits and assessments documented in a traceable way? If nonconformities are found, are they reported through the incident reporting process?

*If you answered yes to all of the above, you are in good shape. If you don't know the answers to some of these questions, it's a good idea to get answers.*

# The hiring of employees and contractors

Does your organization have a formal process in place for the hiring of employees and contractors? Does the process require a background check of your employees and contractors? Is the education of a potential employee or a contractor confirmed? Does your organization confirm that your applicant do not have a criminal record? Does your organization run a financial background on job applicants? Does your organization always contact at least two people from previous work places for recommendation?

*If you answered yes to all of the above, you are in good shape. If you don't know the answers to some of these questions, it's a good idea to get answers. It is worth mentioning that if you didn't answer yes to all of these questions, you may still be in good shape as long as it was an informed decision based on a risk assessment.*

# IT security awareness training

Does your organization routinely provide IT security awareness training, were key parts of IT security are emphasized - including, but not limited to, policies, processes and procedures? Does your organization require all of your employees and contractors to receive this training at least once a year? Does your organization also require your organization's executives to receive this training once a year?

*If you answered yes to all of the above, you're in good shape. If you don't know the answers to some of these questions, it's a good idea to get answers.*

# Termination of employment / contractors

Does your organization have a formal documented process in place for termination of employment? Is it a part of the process to revoke and disable access to all information systems and security areas?

*If you answered yes to all of the above, you are in good shape. If you don't know the answers to some of these questions, it's a good idea to get answers.*

# Reporting

Does your organization have a process in place where executive management and other important stakeholders are informed of the results of internal audits for key controls, including the ones covered in this chapter? Do these results include number of nonconformities discovered and which corrective actions have already been implemented in response to the non-conformities?

*If you answered yes to all of the above, you are in good shape. If you don't know the answers to some of these questions, it's a good idea to get answers.*

# Contractual reporting and monitoring of third parties

Is there a process within your organization, which makes sure to include monitoring and reporting requirements in all contracts with third parties (whether they are a software development company, hosting company, service provider, auditing company, anything else)? Does your organization contractually require software companies to report known security vulnerabilities to you in products that you use? Does your organization contractually require third parties to notify you of security breaches and incidents that relate to their infrastructure or may relate to the services they offer to your organization? Does your organization contractually require your third parties to allow your own organization's internal and external auditors to audit controls, relating to the services they offer to your organization? Does your organization contractually require your third parties to implement the controls referenced in this chapter?

*If you answered yes to all of the above, you're in good shape. If you don't know the answers to some of these questions, it's a good idea to get answers.*

# Change Management

Does your organization have a formal change management process in place (specially for larger changes in the IT environment)? Does the process cover who is required to authorize which changes? Does this process require the following information to be supplied prior to changes being performed?

- Change description
- When is the change scheduled?
- Expected time it will take to perform the change
- Expected downtime of the Information System in question (and potentially related systems)
- Who will perform the changes
- Backup plan (in case we run into problems / change won't work); (e.g. recover from backup)
- Estimated time it will take to revert the change (backup plan)
- How will changes be tested to confirm success?

*If you answered yes to all of the above, you're in good shape. If you don't know the answers to some of these questions, it's a good idea to get answers.*

# Backup management

Does your organization have a formal process in place for performing backups and the recovery of backups? Has this process been approved by top management? Has a backup plan been implemented? Was top management involved in defining and approving the backup frequencies and data retention periods for key information systems? Were the backup frequencies and data retention periods accepted in a formal and traceable way by executive management? Does your organization try to recover key information systems at least once a year from backups? Do their owners confirm the recovered information systems work? Are these recoveries and tests documented in a formal and traceable way?

*If you answered yes to all of the above, you are in good shape. If you don't know the answers to some of these questions, it's a good idea to get answers.*

# Business Continuity Plan (BCP)

Does your organization have a formal BCP in place? Is it based on best practices and international standards? Does your organization's BCP cover how to respond to the most probable risk factors, which may cause a disruption in your business operations? Does your organization's BCP include Recovery Time Objectives (RTO) and Maximum Tolerable Downtime (MTDT) for your key information systems and processes? Does your organization's change management process require the BCP to be updated and maintained as appropriate? Does your organization perform exercises of the BCP at least annually? Are executives involved in parts of the exercises?

*If you answered yes to all of the above, you're in good shape. If you don't know the answers to some of these questions, it's a good idea to get answers.*

# Incident Response Plan

Does your organization have a documented incident response plan in place (for example in the case of a computer break in)? Does your organization's incident response plan require executive management to be informed of breaches or critical security vulnerabilities identified?

*If you answered yes to all of the above, you're in good shape. If you don't know the answers to some of these questions, it's a good idea to get answers.*

# Software Development

Does your organization do any software development? If so, has a secure software development lifecycle been designed and documented (SDLC)? Is it based on international standards (e.g. ISO/IEC 27034) and best practices? Do your organization's employees get regular training in secure software development with a focus on known security vulnerabilities and how to defend against them (e.g. OWASP top 10, SANS CWE top 25)? When software is being developed to communicate data between systems, is there a requirement for those communications to always be encrypted? Are there formal channels, processes and procedures in place to report and handle security vulnerabilities, which are discovered in the software being developed by your organization?

*If you answered yes to all of the above, you are in good shape. If you don't know the answers to some of these questions, you might consider getting answers. I do realize that this part is a bit technical and possibly over complicated, so it's up to you how much information you will request, but answers to the first few questions asked in this section should be known to you.*

# EU General Data Protection Regulation (GDPR)

Does your organization do business with any company or clients located in the EU? If so, are you aware of the potential fines your organization could face in case of non-compliance (up to 4% of annual turnover)? Has your organization hired, or appointed, a Data Protection Officer (DPO)? Has your organization started working towards GDPR compliance?

*If you answered yes to all of the above, you're in good shape. If you don't know the answers to some of these questions, it's a good idea to get answers.*

# ABOUT THE AUTHOR

Svavar Ingi Hermannsson is one of Iceland's leading experts in information security. He has been specializing in IT security and software development for the last 20 years and has held various roles in programming and IT Security consulting with vast experience in penetration testing, vulnerability assessment, code auditing, information security management - including ISO/IEC 27001, PCIDSS and PADSS. These roles include a manager position at KPMG, as well as a CISO position at one of the leading mobile payment application company in Iceland.

Svavar has taught classes at the University of Iceland and the University of Reykjavik.

Svavar was the chairman of the information security focus group at the Icelandic Computer Society from 2007-2012. He has given talks at multiple events in Iceland, the UK, Germany, Ukraine, Sweden and the US, including OWASP, BSides, Hacker Halted Europe and UISGCon.

Svavar is a lifetime member of OWASP and holds various certifications, including CISSP, CISA and CISM.